Talk to ME!
A Child's Insight Into Disability

KATE HINGSTON

First published by Ultimate World Publishing 2021
Copyright © 2021 Kate Elizabeth Hingston

ISBN

Paperback: 978-1-922714-39-8
Ebook: 978-1-922714-40-4

Kate Elizabeth Hingston has asserted her rights under the Copyright, Designs and Patents Act 1988 to be identified as the author of this work. The information in this book is based on the author's experiences and opinions. The publisher specifically disclaims responsibility for any adverse consequences which may result from use of the information contained herein. Permission to use information has been sought by the author. Any breaches will be rectified in further editions of the book.

All rights reserved. No part of this publication may be reproduced, stored in or introduced into a retrieval system, or transmitted in any form, or by any means (electronic, mechanical, photocopying, recording or otherwise) without the prior written permission of the author. Any person who does any unauthorised act in relation to this publication may be liable to criminal prosecution and civil claims for damages. Enquiries should be made through the publisher.

Cover design: Ultimate World Publishing
Layout and typesetting: Ultimate World Publishing
Editors: Maree Hingston and Xavier Ennis
Author photo: Julie Sleeman on Facebook - @Souled.On.Images or Instagram – sleemojules.

Ultimate World Publishing
Diamond Creek,
Victoria Australia 3089
www.writeabook.com.au

Testimonials

"Just awesome! This book really captured the emotions of someone who has a disability, the usual attitudes that kids have towards disability in general, and a simple and positive outcome."

Vinnie Mammoliti
Bachelor in IT and
Person with a Disability

"I've known Kate for a long time, both professionally and personally. I too have worked in disability for a very long time and have seen all too often the humiliation, exclusion and dismissive reactions of people towards those with a disability. This story brings not just hope but actual ways to show how kids can work together to challenge perceptions and change people's reactions. This book can inspire kids to change the future for themselves and their community, as well as building great relationships!"

Megan Phillips
Psychologist

"Kate has always been a passionate advocate for the rights and inclusion of people with a disability of all ages. Through her book 'Talk to ME!' she encourages children (and adults), to think about the barriers that people with a disability face and how they can be part of the solution in creating welcoming and inclusive communities. It is a great read and will no doubt inspire readers into action."

Ann-Maree Davis
Chief Executive Officer
Amicus Group Inc

 Dedication

To my loving husband, Andrew, who supported me to fulfil my dream of writing this children's book, and to my family who support me in so many other ways. A special thanks to my mother-in-law, Maree Hingston, who provided me with some structure and editing (and cake).

To my acquaintance and now friend, Jye Yates, whom I was honoured to interview so that I could have a character based on real life experiences.

To the disability organisations I have been employed in along the way: Department of Human Services (Now, Department of Families, Fairness and Housing), City of Greater Bendigo (Aged and Disability Services), Multiple Sclerosis Australia and Scope who have all provided me with direct

Talk to ME!

and indirect learning experiences. More recently, Melbourne City Mission where I am employed as a Specialist Support Coordinator to implement participants' National Disability Insurance Scheme (NDIS) plans.

Last but not least, to a nursing friend and a past mentor in my early career at DHS (now DFFH), Ann-Maree Davis.

Contents

Testimonials	3
Dedication	5
Introduction	9
Chapter 1: When Tom met Harry	11
Chapter 2: An adventure to remember	17
Chapter 3: You are safe with me Harry	23
Chapter 4: A new friend with wheels	27
Chapter 5: The new kid	31
Chapter 6: The bullies	35
Chapter 7: A smile goes a long way	39
Chapter 8: Tom's idea	45
Chapter 9: Talk to ME	51
Chapter 10: Young minds think alike	57
Chapter 11: Stars are born	61
Chapter 12: Dreams can come true	67
About the Author	71
Acknowledgements	75
Further Testimonials	77
Calls to Action	79

 Introduction

Changing perception and attitudes – whether from nature or nurture from a young age is the idea behind this book. This book, **Talk to ME!**, is a result of my view that there is a lack of general understanding in the community of what it means for a person to live with a disability.

To understand and appreciate how challenging some people's lives are, and ultimately all the things that you or I may take for granted that should not be buried or misunderstood.

I believe acceptance should be taught from a young age so that it becomes an inherent societal norm in our growing population. Therefore, this book has been written for children specifically of primary school age.

Talk to ME!

Characters, Tom, Harry, Ricardo, and Zack all have a different type of disability and I am mindful that there are many other forms of disability that bring greater challenges, however, for the purpose of this book, I have framed these characters to be voiced and delivered from children's perspectives.

In addition, I have cast a real person into this book who preferred me to use his own name; Mister Jye Yates. Jye also hopes that people can gain a greater acceptance of disability from this book and that other kids growing up do not have to endure what he did. Forty years ago, many people, including professionals, focused on a medical model of disability *(which focused on limitations)* as opposed to the social model of disability *(which focuses on adapting to the needs of people with disabilities)*.

Anyone could be born with, or acquire a disability, so please read this book to your young ones and even better, spread the word about **Talk to ME!**

Chapter 1

When Tom met Harry

It was Tom and Harry's first day in a new year at Braveheart Primary School.

Tom was walking very carefully as the ground was uneven and there were things in front of him that he wasn't used to. Unable to see, Tom relied on his other senses and his clever white cane to feel his way. Tom had been using a cane from a young age as he was born without sight and the cane helped him feel what was in front of him.

Harry was wearing a hoodie partly covering his face and he was walking along while watching other kids as he was worried about them staring at him. Harry

When Tom met Harry

was born with a strawberry red birth mark on one side of his face and down his neck. He was very good at hiding it with his clothing. Because he was kind, Harry wished others would be nice to him as well.

In the classroom, the teacher, Miss Honey suggested that the kids pair up and get to know each other. This was a bit scary for both Tom and Harry. Tom couldn't see where everyone was and Harry was timidly covering his face. Tom could hear lots of scurrying around him within the room then silence. Harry just knew no one would want to talk to him, because they never did. Tom and Harry were the only two left without someone to talk to. Miss Honey suggested they sit together and have a chat. Miss Honey would not have known then the friendship that was going to grow from that day.

"Hi, my name is Tom and you might have noticed I have a disability."

"But you are not in a wheelchair," said Harry who thought all people with a disability were in a wheelchair.

"No I'm not, but I am blind" said Tom.

Talk to ME!

"But you are looking straight at me," said Harry, a little bit confused.

"Yes, maybe I am, but I can't see you," said Tom in a voice that sounded as though he had said this many times before.

"What can you see then?" said Harry awkwardly.

"I can't see anything but I can hear by your tone of voice that you are a kind and caring person," said Tom.

"I'm glad you can't see me", said Harry very quietly so the other kids couldn't hear him, "You wouldn't like what you see anyway because I have a big red birth mark on my face."

"That's doesn't bother me. Let's be friends," said Tom.

"Oh, yes, let's be friends Tom. My name is Harry. I really wish more kids were like you."

Talk to ME!

"We are put in situations to build our character... not destroy us."
Nick Vujicic

Chapter 2

An adventure to remember

One day Tom and Harry went to the zoo with their Mums. Harry could describe the animals to Tom so he could imagine what they looked like.

Tom was using his cane with Harry guiding him. Tom could tell they were getting close as he could smell some strange, stinky smells, like the time when his Dad had taken him to a piggery.

Harry said, "This animal has four legs, a nice black tail, it's much bigger than us and it has black and white stripes; it's a zebra, like a horse but with stripes."

Talk to ME!

"Oh, wow! This one is really, really tall and it has a big long neck. It has some spots on it and its mouth can reach the tree tops to eat branches. It's a giraffe." Tom had heard of these animals before through his Mum reading story books to him. His imagination was painting a picture in his mind.

They went past different cages with all types of monkeys. Harry described them while laughing about the funny faces they were pulling and how they were showing off their red bottoms. Tom could hear lots of chatter and screeching noises coming from the area. "Don't get too close, Tom. Monkeys can bite."

Next, they walked past the lions' den. Harry described the lion to Tom, "There is one laying on a big rock, it looks like it has hair all around its face, like a beard. There are other ones too but they don't have a hairy face." They both laughed. They heard a man reading the sign. "African lions can grow up to three metres long from head to tail; they are heavy animals weighing around 150 to 250 kilograms. African lions usually live in prides, groups of ten or fifteen."

"Wow", said Tom "I can't imagine how big that is compared to humans." Then an almighty roar came

An adventure to remember

from the pen, it seemed to give everyone a fright. The lion had stood up, he was pushing out his chest and he was so big. "Phew, let's go Tom."

Tom was thinking how cool this place was and how Harry was very good at describing their surroundings.

A bit further along Harry looked through the glass and saw a snake curled up in ball with a smooth scaly body. Harry was a very good reader and read the facts from the board. "Wow, snakes have a unique anatomy which allows them to swallow and digest large prey." Neither were quite sure what some of the big words meant or even if Harry sounded them right but Harry could tell, Tom was a bit frightened.

Harry hurried Tom away from the snake while guiding him into an enclosure where it felt warm and safe. Harry didn't say a single word this time and waited for Tom's reaction. Tom felt something soft flicker onto his face. He jumped slightly.

Harry said, "Don't be scared, it's a beautiful coloured butterfly." Together they stood in silence, then another butterfly landed on Tom's back and his arm. They stood very still with colourful butterflies

An adventure to remember

of all sizes touching them. They were both smiling while enjoying that moment together. Harry looked around at the butterflies on everyone else. All of Tom's, senses had come alive, his sense of smell, his hearing, and his sense of touch. He was so excited but felt very calm. "You really are a good friend, Harry. What a beautiful place! Let's come here again one day, but we'll avoid that snake!"

Chapter 3

You are safe with me Harry

Harry went over to Tom's house to play. By now they had done some really cool things together and the zoo trip was the best so far.

Since Harry had met Tom he always wondered what it would be like to be blind. He had never really thought about 'disability', and thought it just related to people in wheelchairs. Harry himself had faced his own difficulty with his birthmark, it made him feel disabled because he looked different to everyone else.

Talk to ME!

They were laying on Tom's bedroom floor playing guessing games. Harry asked, "What is it like to be blind?" Tom thought Harry sounded a little bit sad. "I don't know any different, why do you ask? Does it worry you Harry?" "No, Tom, it doesn't worry me, and I like that you can't see me. Does that sound bad? I hope I haven't hurt your feelings, Tom?" "It's okay, Harry, one thing that's good about being blind is all my other senses come to life because I can't see. Mum said I am lucky in some funny kind of way. I didn't know what she meant at first but now I do. Remember when we were at the zoo and the butterflies were landing on us? That was the best feeling in the world, it brought all my senses to life and I felt I didn't need to see them, as I could imagine them. Do you get it now?" "I find that really hard to imagine not being able to see anything," said Harry who was still remembering the butterfly enclosure and how beautiful it was watching all the butterflies everywhere.

They lay quietly for a little while, then Tom had an idea. "Hey, Harry, what if we blindfold you and you could use my cane and then I could guide you around the house?" "Ummm, I'm not sure, Tom. I might trip you up and you might hurt yourself." "No,

Talk to ME!

it will be okay, I know this house well," Tom replied with confidence. "I have a scarf that you could use to put over your eyes, it's in the top drawer." "Okay then, let's give it a go," said Harry. He took the scarf out of the drawer and tied it around his head covering his eyes. "What now? I'm ready, but it's so dark and a bit scary." Tom stood up, grabbed his cane, and passed it to Harry. Harry was feeling scared. Tom sensed his fear and said, "Don't be scared, Harry. I won't let anything happen to you."

Harry grabbed the back of Tom's shirt firmly as he was being led around the house. Tom was counting the steps out loud and telling Harry when they had to turn left or right. From the bedroom to the bathroom, from the bathroom to the lounge room, from the lounge room to the kitchen, from the kitchen to the laundry, counting steps and turns out loud. Harry was amazed that Tom could do this so well. Harry was starting to feel more comfortable while still holding Tom's shirt, but a little looser now. Tom asked, "Are you okay? You're quiet, Harry?" Harry replied, "Yes I'm okay and I'm more glad now you are my friend. You make me feel safe."

Chapter 4

A new friend with wheels

Tom and Harry were at the park one sunny Saturday afternoon, everyone seemed to be out and about. Tom could feel a vibe in the air, he heard the sounds of children playing and dogs barking and he could smell the freshly cut grass. Harry was feeling a lot more confident these days as he'd never really had a friend as special as Tom. Tom was really enjoying hanging out with Harry as well because they had fun together.

Today there was a special event where lots of kids were in wheelchairs and having some kind of race. Harry said, "Let's go and watch. Oh, sorry Tom I didn't mean watch, but come with me so we can

Talk to ME!

cheer them on." Tom used his cane while Harry was by his side guiding him through the crowd.

Harry said, "It's about to start. They are all at a big blow-up start sign. There are some kids with a person to push the wheelchairs and some on their own." A loud starter pistol sounded, and they were off! "'Wow,' said Harry, "look at them go! Oh, sorry Tom, you know what I mean." Tom didn't flinch as he stood enjoying the atmosphere, the noise, the feeling of closeness to people. He smelled their sweat and felt the sensation of the fine hairs on the back of his neck standing up with excitement.

The race was nearly at the end as everyone was screaming and shouting. Then they announced the winner. It was a boy about their age, named Ricardo. Harry described Ricardo to Tom. "He has brown curly hair and he is in a wheelchair. He used his arms to push himself to the finish line, he must be fit. He looks so strong and confident, and he looks like he doesn't have a care in the world."

Tom said, "Do you think we could meet him?" "We could try," said Harry. "What do you think you would

Talk to ME!

say to him?" "Maybe start with 'congratulations'," said Tom. "Hmmm," said Harry. They both chuckled.

As they walked over to Ricardo's new fan club, Tom was holding Harry's shirt while walking through the crowd. Harry started to get conscious of his birthmark and realised how different he might look to strangers. But then he thought, we are all a little bit different. Face, eyes, legs, who cares? We are all people.

When they finally got their turn to congratulate, Ricardo spoke to them with confidence. Ricardo mentioned that he was starting school at the Braveheart Primary School which was the same school as Tom and Harry. They all thought that was great. Tom said, "Our teacher is Miss Honey and she's very nice." Harry and Tom thought that Ricardo was a friendly person, and that it was a shame that more of the kids at school weren't like him. Tom and Harry ended their afternoon with a smile on their faces knowing that things aren't so bad when you have friends.

Chapter 5

The new kid

Tom and Harry were excited and eagerly waiting to see Ricardo on the day he started at their school. Tom asked Harry to keep an eye out for Ricardo. They weren't quite sure what they were going to talk about but just had comfort knowing that he wouldn't treat them any differently like some of the other school kids did.

Ricardo had wheeled himself into the classroom ahead of Miss Honey who said, "I'd like to introduce you to our new student, Ricardo, who has moved from the city." Tom heard a few mean comments and chuckles coming from behind him.

The new kid

Next minute out loud and totally out of character for Harry, he yelled out, "Stop it!" He turned to the class and said, "He is no different from you except he uses a wheelchair for legs, and he won a race last Saturday in his wheelchair, so there!" The teacher nodded, smiling slightly at Harry, then said, "Okay, class, why don't we let Ricardo tell you a little bit about himself? Ricardo, are you happy to do that?" Ricardo said, "Thank you, I would really like that."

"Mum told me that when I was about two years old, I climbed up to the top of my brother's bunk bed. I was jumping up and down on the bed then lost my balance and I fell backwards from the top bunk. I lost the use of my legs and after a long time in hospital, I was given a wheelchair to get around. Mum told me I had a spinal cord injury and she said I was very lucky I didn't die."

The classroom was silent until Harry said, "Thanks, Ricardo. If it's okay to ask, you were able to walk, then you had the accident?" "Yes," said Ricardo." "So, people with all kinds of problems can either be born that way or get them later? So it could happen to anyone then?" "Yes, that's right Harry," said Miss Honey, while Ricardo was nodding yes.

Talk to ME!

Then a little girl named Angela spoke. She said, "Well my brother was born with Autism." Miss Honey said, "Tell us more about that Angela." Everyone was now listening, even the bullies at the back of the class, as they hadn't heard that word before. Angela explained, "He is different in his mind and he thinks in a different way to me. Everything has to be in order, he is really good at facts and he can remember things like all the football player's names and their numbers. He even knows the Captains of every team." One of the bullies yelled out, "Well, duh, everyone knows that!" "Yeah, but he can also name every player in the AFL in their order of number and, he's only ten years old," said Angela proudly. Miss Honey said, "All this is very interesting, although I think that is enough on this subject for today. We will make a special time to talk about differences and maybe even invite a speaker to the class."

This got Tom thinking that not many people really understand disability. Tom wanted to do something about this but he didn't know what. Tom was pleased that he might have another new friend in Angela.

Chapter 6

The bullies

Ricardo had been going to the school now for about two weeks. Tom and Harry were like his best mates. They all got along well and were able to help each other if they needed. Sometimes Harry would give Ricardo a push up the ramp for fun, or if they were hurrying after the bell rang, and sometimes Tom would be able to let either of them know when he sensed they were being stared at. This was more often lately as the class bullies were always staring and saying mean things.

The school day had come to an end and as usual, the three boys were leaving the school across the football ground to get to the bus. The bullies had run ahead of them and were hiding behind a bench where the footy players sit.

Tom was being more focused than usual. He was being quiet, like he was listening. At one stage while walking towards the football ground Tom said, "Shhhh." Next minute they heard bully one say, "Not so tough now are ya, wheels for legs?" The other bullies laughed out loud and then they started to throw stones at the boys who were trying to duck for cover. Poor Tom didn't have a chance as he wasn't able to see the stones coming at him. Then bully two ran around behind Tom and kicked his cane away. Harry, while trying to help Tom, got knocked to the ground. Tom dropped down and covered his head and face. Bully three was now kicking Harry and calling him 'scar face'. Ricardo tried to protect his new friends by ramming the bullies with his chair but it was just too hard. Ricardo really hated that he couldn't walk. He wanted to stand up and help his mates.

From a distance they could hear chanting from bigger kids, "Fight, fight, fight!" Angela had seen what was happening and ran back to the classroom to get the teacher's help. Principal McGregor and

Talk to ME!

Miss Honey came running through the school gate to the oval with Angela behind them. The bullies scrambled as quickly as they could to get out of sight. Miss Honey ran to Harry as he lay on the ground while Mr. McGregor fetched Tom's cane from the oval. Ricardo was just sitting in his chair barely able to speak, as he was in shock. Harry was injured and complaining of a sore arm. It was swollen and he couldn't move it.

Mr. McGregor called an ambulance. Then their parents were called and Harry was taken to hospital. Harry lay in the hospital bed that night with a broken arm and bruising. His body was sore and he was feeling very sad. He and his friends had been hurt by the bullies and he thought they shouldn't be able to get away with it.

Angela was also worried about the three boys in her class and was so glad her brother hadn't been bullied like that. As Tom lay wide awake that night he thought, this is very serious, we must do something so others understand how we feel. They can't treat us like that!

🦋 Chapter 7 🦋

A smile goes a long way

Miss Honey, as promised, had organised a guest speaker. She introduced him, his name was Mr. Yates. Mr. Yates was in an electric wheelchair and he used a knob on the side to make it move along. Miss Honey announced some of his achievements. He had many trophies and medals in a number of sports and was recognised in the balloon football league hall of fame. She also said he visits schools and teaches young kids in wheelchairs how to play that sport.

The kids had some questions already prepared. "What was it like to grow up with a disability?" said Angela who had some idea. Although her brother's disability was different, she was interested.

A smile goes a long way

Mr. Yates explained. "Back about forty years ago it was harder than it is now because a lot of people thought a person with a disability should be locked away and hidden. When I was one year old, I was diagnosed with Cerebral Palsy. The doctor said, "He won't walk, he won't talk, he'll never be any good for anything, put him in a home and forget about him, or you can take him home and put him in a bean bag – He will be a bean bag baby! But, the doctor was wrong and here I am today living independently and talking to you kids, thanks to my Mum.

"I had lots of therapy and operations, my legs were in and out of plaster. I had speech therapy to help me get my words out. They wanted me to learn sign language but Mum insisted I learn to speak. And here I am speaking to you now. It might seem like I'm slurring or even sound a bit drunk, but I am not and I can understand everything that goes on around me. Some people think because I talk a bit strangely, I don't understand things and need to ask others around me to make choices for me. That really gets under my skin because I can talk and think for myself.

Talk to ME!

"Mum said when I was four years old and unable to walk, she had me in a pusher and a lady rudely said to me. "You are a lazy boy. Why don't you get out and walk for your mother?" Mum firmly answered her, "Well he would if he could but he has Cerebral Palsy." Apparently, the lady felt really badly that she said that (once she knew the reason I was in a pusher). Another similar thing happened when I was in my smaller power chair and I had my primary school uniform on. A lady came up in the shopping centre and says, "Isn't that our local school uniform?" Mum answered, "Yes". The lady then said, "Well, isn't he lucky… in a wheelchair?"

"When I think about it now, I wonder if I had two heads or something, did I look that bad? "What do you all think about what she said?"

Bully one, with a grin on his face said, "You've only got one head but you don't sound normal." Miss Honey went red in the face and made him go to the back of the class and ordered him not to say another word. Maybe he thought he would get a reaction from his mates but they were too scared to say anything.

A smile goes a long way

Mr. Yates continued, "I went to high school and I had a lot of great mates who would stick up for me. These kids were my neighbours and grew up with me so they had an understanding from a young age. They are all still my friends now and we catch up regularly. Because I was accepted by my peers, the teachers learned from them and accepted me as well.

"If a person is in a wheelchair, it doesn't mean they can't communicate, if a person's speech is a bit slurred, it doesn't mean they are silly. If a person can't see, it doesn't mean they can't hear. When it comes down to it, we all have feelings, with or without a disability. In other words, treat others how you would like to be treated.

"So, what are you going to do next time you see someone who looks or even talks a little bit differently?"

"You could smile at them," said Angela.
"You could say 'Hi'," said Abdul.
"You could treat them nice," said Lin-lee.
"You could ask if they need help," said Ricardo.
"You could ask them their name," said Penny.

Talk to ME!

"And you could even say 'how are you?'" said Miss Honey.

"Yes, all of those are very good answers and I hope you all have a better understanding of what it is like for someone to live with a disability. Saying something positive is better than saying nothing at all. Thanks for listening to me," said Mr. Yates.

Chapter 8

Tom's idea

For many weeks now, Tom had been thinking how he and his mates could help others understand and accept people with a disability. What had happened to them at school was probably happening all over the world. Mr. Yates had told them all the things that happened to him as a kid even though it was a bit better now, but still it was not good enough.

Mr. Yates had been to the school to talk about his own experiences and these days he travels around and supports young kids with a disability. He encourages them to get involved with sport while spreading the word and sharing his own stories. Tom thought that Mr. Yates really helped everyone

Talk to ME!

in the classroom to understand his message, even the bullies. Tom felt sad for what Mr. Yates and his Mum had been through.

Tom wanted to come up with an idea or a saying that people would remember. He thought if the message could be taught early in life then those young people could take it home to their own families.

Tom thought some of these ideas might work.

"Don't look at me that way."
"I am a human being."
"We are human, but not all the same."
"Same, but a little bit different."
"We are all human, but different."
"Eyes, face, legs, who needs them?"

Tom was starting to get angry with himself. Why couldn't he think of something that could be catchy, something that people would remember? He wasn't really happy with anything he had come up with so far, so he decided to talk to Harry and Ricardo about his ideas. After all, they had experienced discrimination too.

Tom's idea

Tom was keen to have himself and others heard; he had never been so focused about anything in his whole eight years of life. As Tom lay awake, he couldn't help but think about Mr. Yates' friends at high school and how they are still good friends. He went off to sleep with a smile knowing what great friends he had and dreamed about how their friendship might grow. As he drifted off to sleep he was thinking about the perfect place to meet up with his friends and how grateful he felt to have them in his life.

Talk to ME!

"Just because a man lacks the use of his eyes doesn't mean he lacks vision."
Stevie Wonder

Chapter 9

Talk to ME

Tom, Harry and Ricardo's mothers had got to know each other better since the bullying incident. They had arranged for the boys to meet at the shopping centre while they went shopping. Their mums knew they needed some time together and gave them each ten dollars to spend.

This was the first time the boys had actually caught up to talk about what had happened that day after school. They talked about Harry's arm because it was still in plaster. Harry told them it was getting better and the bruising had almost gone.

Talk to ME!

They spoke about what had happened to the bully boys. Mr. McGregor had asked the bullies' parents to come in to speak to him. After this some changes were made in the classroom. The bullies were separated from each other and they were all made to write letters of apology to Tom, Harry, and Ricardo. Tom heard that bully three who kicked Harry, was made to stay in his bedroom and do homework for two weeks and not see his friends outside of school. He wasn't even allowed to play football on Saturdays. The bullies had behaved better at school lately, especially after Mr. Yates came to speak.

The three friends had been sitting at the table waiting for someone to take their orders. A young waiter was taking people's orders, but it seemed to be taking forever and it looked as if the waiter was avoiding them. Harry said to the waiter as politely as he could, "Excuse me, are you going to come and ask us what we want?" The waiter's face turned the colour pink and he seemed nervous. He said, "Oh yeah, just a minute okay?" He then nervously came over and said to Harry. "What do you want?" Harry said, "A chocolate milkshake please." The waiter then asked Harry, "What does your friend in the wheelchair want?" Harry replied, "Ask him yourself. He can speak, you know." "Oh," said the waiter. Ricardo said, "Yes, talk to me. Oh, I'll save you the trouble, I'll have a banana milkshake." Tom was staring blankly into the air waiting to be asked. The waiter said, "Okay, well, is that it?" Tom said, "Just because I can't see you it doesn't mean you can ignore me. I'll have a banana milk shake too, thanks." The waiter hurried off, whispering to the lady making the drinks, "One chocolate and two banana milkshakes for the freaks over on table six."

Because Tom's hearing was so much more sensitive than the others, he heard his every word, which really upset him. What the waiter said was so hurtful. He seemed to have no idea that he had hurt anyone's feelings or about treating people with respect. Tom thought it was a good time to talk to his friends about people in general not accepting them for who they are.

Tom really wanted to come up with a saying. He told his friends his ideas, even though he didn't think they were very good. This got the others thinking as well.

Talk to ME

Ricardo said, "What about, 'Love me for who I am,' or, 'I can communicate if you'll let me?'" Or maybe it could say, 'I'm different but the same as you,' 'We are normal just like you,' or… 'Talk to me!'" Tom's mind was racing fast, that rude waiter and Ricardo's reaction on to him had given Tom another idea. How about, just 'Talk to me!' "Yes, I like it, 'Talk to me!'" said Ricardo out loud.

They had just finished their milkshakes and their mums had returned ready to take them home. "See you both at school on Monday," said Harry, "we can talk more about this then." You are both great friends."

Chapter 10

Young minds think alike

Monday came around quickly. The bullies had all been seated apart in the classroom and were behaving better. They must have really got into trouble with their parents! Angela and her friend Olivia had started to hang out with the boys as well. Liv, as she liked to be called, was a nice girl. She was one of the kids in the classroom who had never been mean to them. Now they were a group of five.

At play time the boys had shared their idea of a 'saying' with the girls and asked them if they had any ideas about getting the word out. Liv asked, "What about a poster or a sticker to put on cars

Young minds think alike

and trucks and motorbikes? I've seen cars with stickers on them; that would be really cool!" "Hey," said Angela, "we could get my brother Zack to design it, he's really good at art." All the boys were nodding, smiling, and thinking to themselves, "This could actually work!"

Harry said, "We could also get the saying, or whatever we are calling it, a motto or a slogan into the school newsletter." Tom said, "Let's call it a slogan. I've heard that before on TV. Any other ideas?"

"All that sounds good," said Ricardo, "But what about someone to explain what it means? We know what it means because we live with it. I'm the boy in the wheelchair who people are too scared to talk to. I'm sick of it." Tom replied, "Okay, Ricardo, we hear you, it sucks doesn't it?" They were all nodding together. "Maybe," said Harry, "Mr. Yates could help us, he goes around educating people about accepting disability."

"Okay then, all these ideas are great and now we all have jobs to do," said Tom.

Talk to ME!

"Angela, can you please ask your brother Zack if he could design our slogan, 'Talk to ME!' I won't be able to see it so you all have to be the judges." "Ricardo can you please contact Mr. Yates? Miss Honey should be able to help you. Harry can you please contact the people who write the school newsletter and see if they can help? My dad's friend works as a printer. I'll ask Dad if he can contact him."

"This is fun, I hope we can get the message out," said Angela. "Maybe we will all be famous," said Liv. They all chuckled. "It doesn't matter if we are famous or not, at least we are all friends," said Harry. Tom had a little smile on his face, feeling more positive than he had felt in a long while.

 **Chapter 11**

Stars are born

Everyone had been very busy these past few months doing their bit to get the final slogan and make up the first of the car bumper stickers and posters. Zack was able to get the drawings done over a few weeks with a couple of tweaks to get to the finished product. Tom's dad's friend was able to help print the final drawing.

Miss Honey had taken on supporting this special project so that she could help her students. Harry thought because the teachers see first-hand how cruel kids can be, they were keen to help. The school was happy to put the slogan in the monthly newsletter and also to dedicate an article about disability each month.

The message was getting out that everyone needs to have more acceptance and understanding of people with a disability. The newspaper article, the monthly stories in the newsletter, the posters and bumper stickers, were all helping to get the message across. The aim was to help unaware kids and even grownups, like the young waiter at the shopping centre, who were too scared to talk to people who may appear to be a little different.

Mr. Yates promised that at all his future events he would tell the story of the young kids at the Braveheart Primary School and how they made up the slogan, **Talk to ME!** He took some posters and bumper stickers to give out to people. He also promised to keep in touch.

Tom's dad's friend had a connection with the local newspaper and was able to get the printing company to donate some money. Tom had the insight to push all of this but he couldn't have done it alone, he thought back to how it all came about.

Stars are born

Firstly, Harry and he were sat together in class that day by Miss Honey when no-one wanted to talk to them. This started off their friendship. That led to going to the zoo and their catch-up at Tom's house when Harry explored what it was like to be blind and put all of his trust in Tom. Then they met Ricardo at the park race, and he ended up being in their class at school and they all instantly became friends. After that they were beaten up by the bullies, and Harry ended up in hospital. Then that waiter treated them like they didn't exist. Miss Honey and Mr. McGregor were a great help by splitting the bullies up and making them apologise. Most importantly, Mr. Yates had been invited to speak to the class and talk about his experiences growing up with a disability.

Also, Tom thought back to all the mean and silly comments he heard wherever he went. All of these things put together made him more focused on doing something about it. In a way he was grateful about the way it all happened, as it got him thinking, and that's just what was needed.

Stars are born

Because of this, they had come together on this special day for the newspaper article. This was a proud day for them all. "Okay," said the cameraman, "Smile and show me how proud you are." Miss Honey, Mr. McGregor, Liv, Angela, Zack and a few other kids were also in the photo and happy to be part of this special day. The children all hoped that their friendships would last for a lifetime.

"Once you choose hope, anything's possible."
Christopher Reeve

 **Chapter 12**

Dreams can come true

The three boys and their new friends were now pretty well-known, at least to their own school and the locals in their town. Their popularity had grown and nearly every kid wanted to be their friend.

Tom could sense a different vibe in the air at school. Harry was feeling less self-conscious and Ricardo seemed to have a bit more push in his arms. Liv and Angela had gone from being unknown in the school to being popular. Zack was getting a lot more respect from people in his class and he had been asked by Mr. McGregor to design an advertising logo for their upcoming inter-school sports day. It seemed that things were looking up for everyone.

Talk to ME!

The word was out in the community. People were talking in the streets about the Braveheart Primary School becoming more inclusive and accepting of people with a disability. Bumper stickers were on the back of most of the local cars and their posters had been seen in supermarkets, chemists, the community hall and the police station.

Mr. McGregor had a request from a nearby primary school for the group of six – Tom, Harry, Ricardo, Liv, Angela, and Zack to speak about their experiences and how the whole idea came about. The other school was having some similar issues with bullying behaviour. Miss Honey was asked to help them organise how they could present the information for the talk. Who knows where this would lead?

School wasn't so bad anymore, especially now that they had many new friends who accepted them for who they were. Every day at school was a new day and a better experience.

However, they all knew that there was a lot more to be done outside of their school and in the wider community but, along with all the good work Mr. Yates was doing, they had made a good start.

Talk to ME!

None of this could have been achieved without their friends, beginning with the day when Tom met Harry!

 About the Author

Kate Hingston was born and raised in Castlemaine, Victoria and moved to Bendigo in 1996 after her husband tragically died. As a nurse and mother of three young children, she decided to further her career in the human services industry where she gained her Bachelor of Social Work degree in 2001.

Kate always considered herself a 'glass half-full' type of person and always wanted to be more creative in her writing. She joined a six-week creative writing course which inspired her creativity in poetry. This led her to write a book of poetry, but only four copies were printed, one for each of her children and one for herself.

Kate is the first to admit that she has always been a 'gonna' ("gonna do this" and "gonna do that").

Talk to ME!

Heading towards sixty years of age, she figured it was about time that she was 'gonna' do something about it, so she created her first children's book about a subject passionate to her heart.

Kate has worked within the human services industry for the last forty three years, initially, as a Nurse where she witnessed ageing and frailty and people coming to terms with disabilities caused through accidents or self-harm. This led her to her career in working with people with disabilities.

As a social worker she has seen first-hand so much discrimination and disempowerment suffered by people with a disability. Kate has moved in-and-out of various positions within the industry, all the while noticing a common theme: people's limited acceptance and understanding of 'disability'. She believes that the often negative or patronising language, or more often the white noise, is a result of people who are actually afraid of what they don't know.

Kate acknowledges that education and greater understanding will bring a greater insight into acceptance of disability. She thought, "What better

About the Author

way to communicate this than through a child's eyes?" This is how 'Talk to ME!' came about. Kate would also like to share a valuable resource in the Call to Action section below which may help adults to explain these messages to children.

 Acknowledgements

This book was inspired by all the persons I have met with a disability and the struggles they can have with everyday life. This book acknowledges the persons who work in the area to support, encourage and build capacity. Within this context I hope that this sends you or your child an educated and positive message.

Further Testimonials

"So insightful on many levels. I think this will be a cornerstone on children's understanding and confidence. I see many more brilliant books stemming from this very sound and illustrative text."

Toni Will
Bachelor of Science, Graduate Diploma Applied Science,
Master of Psychology in Health Psychology and living with Multiple Sclerosis

"Early intervention is identified as vitally important to help change a child's developmental path and improve outcomes, particularly in the field of disability in its varied forms.

Talk to ME!

"Kate's passion to promote the rights of people with disability has impressed me for many years and I am delighted that she has taken this step, as I view 'Talk to ME!' as the ultimate in early intervention.

"Educating children about the broad spectrum of ability and disability and how to support all people to be the best person they can be and to take a stand against discrimination is fundamentally important.

"'Talk to ME!' describes in the most delightful way what disability is, how it impacts on people's lives and opens the conversation to very young people to help break down the barriers and discrimination that remains a pervasive obstacle to people with disabilities. It has the power to improve outcomes for many people with disabilities by changing the attitudes of the youngest generation, and the ones that come after.

"'Talk to ME!' deserves a place on every young person's bookshelf, in every Primary School and Municipal Library."

Kate MacRae
Disability Advocate

Learn more: https://idpwd.org/key-terms/

Check out this website for inclusive language and terms related to a social model of disability.

www.ingramcontent.com/pod-product-compliance
Lightning Source LLC
Chambersburg PA
CBHW040242130526
44590CB00049B/4174